AF601641

The Swiss Solution:

Using Switzerland For Completely Legal Secrecy and Asset Protection

by

Nicholas van Rijn

Books for Business
New York - Hong Kong

The Swiss Solution: Using Switzerland For Completely Legal Secrecy and Asset Protection

by Nicholas van Rijn

ISBN 0-89499-028-4

Reprint of the 1994 edition with some 2001 updates

Books for Business
New York - Hong Kong

http://www.businessbooksinternational.com

Contents

Introduction

This report was written for North American investors who want to gain an extra measure of safety, without sacrificing performance, for at least a portion of their hard-earned wealth. Contrary to the western mystique surrounding a "secret Swiss bank account," this report was **not** written for jet-set international traders who want to make a fast buck, or for criminals who want to hide or launder money, or just for those with several million dollars or more to invest.

This report is aimed at the typical mature American investor who has worked a lifetime to save toward a comfortable retirement, yet who fears the unknown effect of a unique combination of financial problems in America today: inflation (or deflation), bank and S&L closings, stock market uncertainty, record budget deficits, insurance company failures, a sluggish U.S. economy, high taxes and an increasingly repressive government which may rob you of a fair chance to enjoy your wealth.

In seven brief chapters, we'll outline an easy plan for getting started on the road to greater safety and financial success by using Swiss diversification.

1 In Chapter One, you'll learn the fascinating history and current situation in Switzerland, and learn why it's still the world's safest haven for your money.

2 In Chapter Two, you'll learn why diversification between countries is no longer just a luxury -- it is essential.

3 Chapter Three will introduce you to the wide menu of Swiss investments available.

4 Chapter Four examines the Swiss insurance industry, even safer than the famed Swiss banks.

4 Chapter Five will examine the latest, most flexible Swiss investment plan available today, called the Swiss Asset Protection Certificate.

5 Chapter Six examines the Swiss banking system and Swiss secrecy laws.

6 Chapter Seven will get you started investing in Switzerland today.

As you begin to think about investing internationally, you'll need to put aside everything you thought you ever knew about investing and the power of money. The first step is to get beyond any lingering uncertainty that a "foreign" investment is complicated, unsafe or unpatriotic. That's why the first chapter involves a trip to Switzerland and an introduction to how the Swiss respect, and protect, your money.

Chapter One

Introduction to Switzerland

"We will attack no one, participate in no war, will make no alliance, and will defend ourself."

-- The Swiss code of neutrality, as first drafted in 1515

In this opening chapter, let us take a brief tour of Switzerland, but not the traditional tour of the majestic Alps; clean, small cities; picturesque farms and efficient factories. We would like to show you the Switzerland of the mind and spirit, from seven major angles -- the history, politics, financial privacy, national economy, work ethic, currency and defense. Each of these will help you understand why Switzerland remains the world's safest depository for a portion of one's wealth.

A Brief History of Switzerland

The first recorded visitor to the mountainous enclave of Switzerland (then called Helvetia) described the Helvetii people as "rich in gold but peaceable."

Not much has changed since that description in the first century BC, by the Greek writer, Poseidonius. The country still trades more gold than any other nation, holds the greatest amount of gold per capita, and is the only nation which still backs its currency with gold. The Swiss are still noted for their "peaceable" neutrality -- which comes about because they are well armed against any invader foolish enough to risk invading the Swiss national fortress (more on that later).

Over 2,000 years ago, the Romans gained peaceful control of the Alpine terrain and built excellent roads, even over Alpine passes, and beautiful cities. The early Swiss folk adopted Latin as their language and, to this day, some Alpine communities (4% of the people) speak a Swiss version of Latin, called Romansch.

By the late 13th Century, the hunters in the highlands agreed together to resist all outside invaders, and the nation of Switzerland was born. Three woodland states (or "cantons," as the Swiss call them) -- Uri, Schwyz and Unterwalden -- secretly met on August 1, 1291 on a lakeside meadow and swore a solemn Oath of Confederation *(Bundesbrief)*, which provided for mutual assistance among the valley cantons, by "all strength and means." These first three cantons soon brought several other cantons into their "Everlasting League," and formed a perpetual alliance of Swiss cantons under the rule of law, rather than violence.

Within a generation, the Swiss were put to the test and were found to be true to their word. In 1315, foreign attackers on Lake Lucerne were turned away by Swiss "mercenaries" -- hurling boulders from the mountain slopes and using their legendary archery skills. The attackers were completely defeated. The Swiss reputation as fighters spread far and wide, and soon the Pope hired Swiss guards to protect the Vatican, where Swiss Guards have stood continuously since 1506.

Official Swiss neutrality began in the year 1515. After a costly war with the French, Swiss leaders proclaimed, "We will attack no one, participate in no war, will make no alliance, and will defend ourself." Swiss neutrality was officially sanctioned by several international treaties from that point onward, including the Treaty of Westphalia in 1648, the Congress of Vienna in 1815, and the Treaty of Versailles in 1919, following World War I.

Since 1515, no nation has been able to subdue the Swiss, although Napoleon "made a gift of a new constitution" to the Swiss people in the early 19th Century. But soon after Napoleon's final defeat at Waterloo in 1815, the Swiss went back to completely decentralized cantonal rule, until the Federal constitution of 1848 set up a small but weak central government, and a capital in Berne.

The Principle of Neutrality Protects All Wealth, Equally

In the last 700 years, the Swiss have sometimes had to fight to protect their land, but they have never been the aggressor, nor signed an alliance with any aggressor nations. This principle of neutrality is important toward understanding why the Swiss excel at the preservation of individual wealth. Your wealth simply cannot, and will not, be held hostage in Switzerland. By staying out of international conflicts and maintaining strict neutrality, Switzerland has become a refuge for capital from all over the world.

Swiss neutrality is not a passive, theoretical position. The Swiss have a heavily armed neutrality. For instance, Switzerland posted troops at its borders in both World Wars this century, but, having no military allies or international entanglement, the Swiss were not drawn into either of those World Wars.

Swiss neutrality continued after World War II, when the federal parliament called upon the people to ratify Switzerland's membership in the United Nations -- a very popular idea in the rest of the world. But the Swiss people, in a national plebiscite, overwhelmingly voted against joining the U.N. Instead, Switzerland became a neutral site for much of the U.N.'s peace keeping efforts. For decades, Geneva was the site of Soviet/U.S. arms control negotiations, and for the neutral services of the International Red Cross.

Swiss Political Stability

Can you name the President of Switzerland? Probably not. Even if you're well informed on current affairs and know the rulers of most European nations, you're likely never to have seen the name of the Swiss leader, because there is no single leader of the Swiss people. The Swiss are not professional politicians. Only the seven-member Federal Council consists of professional politicians. All others serve only briefly and as an avocation to their main professions.

The Presidency is a rotating office among the seven-member Federal Council, and his name is hardly known in Switzerland, or anywhere else for that matter. The Swiss federal government has always been weak, by design, and the Swiss want to keep it that way. The Federal Assemblies meet only four times a year, in sessions that last only two or three weeks. In fact, the Swiss central government has been described as being "in permanent recess."

The People Rule, Through the Referendum and Initiative

Switzerland is governed at the local level, in each of 26 cantons (made up of 23 full cantons and three half cantons), and over 3,000 municipalities. More than anywhere else on earth, the people rule the rulers, through local control of nearly everything we associate with "government." And when the national government (parliament or national council) exceeds its mandate, the people can easily bring the central government back into line. (Don't you wish that were possible with the U.S. Congress?)

For instance, consider these powers the people possess in Switzerland:

Amendments to the constitution require the direct approval of the voters before they are passed. Unlike the U.S., where state legislatures have the final vote on Constitutional amendments, the people must approve them in Switzerland.

The initiative gives the people the right to contribute directly to the governing process. With 100,000 signatures (just 2% of the voting population), a proposal enters the federal electorate to be voted on. This way, the people help make their own laws. (They also vote for their own teachers, judges and priests!)

The referendum is the most important safeguard of all. If only 50,000 voters desire it (about 1% of the voting age population), any law passed by the government must be submitted to the entire electorate for ultimate approval. If more than 50% of the voters oppose the law in a general election, it is rescinded. And any change in the Constitution is automatically subject to a referendum.

How does this referendum process work to safeguard investor freedoms? Swiss voters can usually be counted on to automatically vote against any measure that increases the government's control, or calls for more fiscal spending.

For example, here are various referenda the Swiss have voted against:

- Not to reduce the work week from 44 to 40 hours.
- Not to establish a uniform rate of taxation for all cantons (some cantons have an extremely low tax rate).
- Not to levy any "soak the rich" taxes on high-income wage earners.
- Not to allow the federal government to run deficits.
- Not to give the federal government "temporary" authority to raise taxes (or run deficits) during times of low economic growth.

- Not to allow laws to increase yearly paid holidays from three to four weeks.
- Not to reduce the minimum age for receiving benefits under the National Old Age Pension Plan.
- Not to give workers authority over management in running corporations.

Because the legislature can be so easily overruled by the people, politicians don't try to enact any new legislation which does not have the support of the bulk of responsible Swiss citizens. Powers not expressly delegated to the federal level remain at the cantonal level. There has never been a strong enough Swiss federal government to take away these cantonal powers.

There is no welfare state mentality among the populace. Support of the poor is primarily a concern of the family, not of the central government. Whenever any legislator floats a welfare-type issue -- like mandating more taxes, starting a minimum-wage program, relaxing Swiss privacy laws, or any other "non-Swiss" trend -- the people quickly vote the law down, usually by a large majority.

These are precisely the types of laws the U.S. Congress has already passed, or is considering, but the Swiss have the right to say no to costly laws like these.

The Swiss central bank is also controlled by the people, more than any other central bank on earth. The Swiss National Bank was founded late in the country's history, in 1906. It is beholden to the people as a joint stock company with a number of institutional and individual shareholders. Any Swiss resident can become a co-owner of the Swiss central bank by owning shares in its stock, which is traded openly over the Swiss stock exchange.

Switzerland as a Financial Privacy Haven

Swiss bankers have served as financiers to the crowned heads of Europe as far back as the Middle Ages. For over 250 years, the Swiss have served as investment bankers to all of Europe -- commoners as well as kings -- and for the last century, Swiss investment services have spanned the globe, with offices on every continent, serving individual investors as well as institutions.

Banking across borders came naturally to the Swiss because of the small size of the nation and its central location to four major nations which border it -- France, Germany, Italy and Austria (which was once the hub of the Austro-Hungarian Empire). Through wars, natural disasters and hyper-inflations, the Swiss have managed to safeguard the wealth of the world. Despite being near the center of history's greatest wars, natural disasters and hyperinflations, Switzerland has stood firm as an oasis of financial sanity.

What is the secret? Switzerland is the only nation in the eastern hemisphere that has never imposed exchange controls on capital outflows. That means no one who has ever invested in Switzerland has been prevented by Swiss government measures from taking his money out again. The probability of Swiss exchange controls in the future is about as close to zero as anything is possible to be.

That's because Swiss financial institutions are a reflection of the general Swiss attitude of respect for private ownership and financial stewardship. Money in Switzerland is a very important matter, and also a very private matter. Open discussion of finances is considered in extremely bad taste, unlike in America, where it seems to me that many people talk openly about their investments, their salary, the value of their home, and even their "secret" overseas bank account!

As a result of its superior respect for financial privacy, Switzerland has the world's safest banks, with more banks per capita than any other major nation -- over 5,000 banks, or one bank for every 1,300 Swiss citizens -- a density of banks encountered nowhere else in the world. Switzerland leads the Western world in per capita savings, but most Swiss bank accounts reflect international deposits. The combined balance sheet total of all Swiss banks -- over 500 billion Swiss francs (about $350 billion, or more than $50,000 per Swiss citizen) -- exceeds the country's Gross National Product by double!

Swiss Financial Privacy -- By Law and Tradition

The Swiss are private by law, as well as tradition. After the election of the Nazis to power in Germany in 1933, the uncertain political future of Europe posed a threat to Swiss independence. To counter these dangers, banking secrecy laws were introduced in 1934, providing a financial haven for current or future refugees in Europe. All bank accounts come under the Swiss Banking Law of 1934, which made strict secrecy the law of the land, heavily punished if violated.

The Bank Secrecy Act of 1934 made it a crime for a bank officer or employee to reveal any information about the customer's account to a third party without the written permission of the customer. Bank officers or employees are further prohibited from disclosing, even to the Swiss government, the existence or contents of any bank account. Bank employees are covered under the law, even after they have left the bank or the banking business. A violation is punishable by a prison term of up to six months and/or a fine of up to 50,000 Swiss francs. Even if the disclosure is by negligence, the fine ranges up to 30,000 Swiss francs.

Thus, banking secrecy is a contractual duty of the bank to the client, and not a "policy" of the bank which can change under different management. The Swiss authorities have resolutely stood firm on this legal concept, even in the face of great foreign pressure. In 1984, Swiss citizens emphatically voted down an initiative to repeal the banking secrecy laws. And there is no question that they intend to vote to preserve privacy continually in the future.

The 1934 Swiss privacy law saved many lives, particularly German Jews in the 1930s, some of whom kept enough money in Switzerland to escape with their lives. Swiss bankers resisted any Nazi subterfuge to penetrate the secrecy of those accounts. And after the war, the U.S. government held all Swiss assets in the U.S. hostage, as leverage to get information out of Swiss banks about Nazi war criminals, but the Swiss remained adamant about protecting privacy.

Swiss banks will sometimes divulge account information to outside authorities, but only if a Swiss law is broken. This does not include any kind of tax crimes or foreign exchange transactions, which are not considered a crime in Switzerland. To further protect individual depositors, all Swiss taxes due on Swiss bank accounts are sent to the government in a lump sum, in a single check for all accounts, without revealing the name or size of any single account.

Swiss banks are also ultra-safe in their financial practices. Many Swiss banks have a liquidity basis of 100% or more, which is almost unheard of in other nations. That's because private Swiss banks do not use deposits from one client to make risky loans to another, either locally or on the international lending market. Swiss banks are full service investment banks. They offer all the standard banking services, like checking and savings accounts, plus professional services, such as stock and commodity brokerage service and investment account management.

Economic Stability in Switzerland

When most people think of Switzerland, they picture the Alps, clocks, chocolates and perhaps even the sound of alpenhorn music. But Switzerland is not primarily a rural, agricultural economy. If you've visited Switzerland, you probably remember the cleanliness and efficiency, the sense of expecting everything to work the way it is supposed to work.

Consider these basic facts about the Swiss economy:

- Per capita income is $27,750 per year -- the highest in the Western world.
- Unemployment is only 0.5% of the labor force, or about 16,500 people.
- Inflation has been historically low, although it is a little higher at the moment.
- 35% of Swiss jobs are in manufacturing, second to Germany in the west.

- Agriculture employs only 5%; services account for most jobs -- 60%.
- Switzerland enjoys a $10 billion current account surplus.
- The Swiss economy grew an average 2.8% over the last four years.

Swiss factories produce some of the world's best precision instruments, railroad locomotives, generators, turbines, machine tools, aluminum, steel, textile machinery, chemicals and pharmaceuticals in the world. Leading Swiss exports include refined precious metals, machinery and parts, and fine Swiss watches, followed by pharmaceuticals. The Swiss tourist industry is the leading service sector, so the Swiss have found it to their advantage to be among the most hospitable hoteliers and restaurateurs in Europe.

Switzerland is the wealthiest nation, per capita, in the Western world, with about $28,000 per person in GNP, compared to second-place Japan, at $23,319. In Europe, the Scandinavian nations earn around $21,000 per person, followed by Germany (not counting the former East Germans) at $19,939, and then $19,733 in the U.S. -- placing America eighth among Western industrialized nations.

The wealth of Switzerland is all the more amazing when you consider that they have almost no natural resources. More than one quarter of Switzerland is completely barren, unfit for human habitation. The remaining land is virtually devoid of natural resources -- no gold, no oil, no coal. Switzerland has no ports for shipping, and the only outlet by water is down the Rhine River from Basel. That path takes a shipper along the borders of four other countries. (Clearly, it pays to maintain neutrality, to insure safe passage.)

Switzerland is small, even by European standards. The entire nation contains only 15,941 square miles -- only about two-thirds the size of West Virginia. Like West Virginia, most of Switzerland is high mountain terrain (but -- unlike West Virginia -- Switzerland has no coal). On top of that, the population is small and remarkably diverse, speaking four major languages and practicing several major religions. By all rights, the Swiss should have long ago dissolved into the Appalachia of Europe, populated by warring clans of "hillbillies."

Because of its size and location, and its voracious import needs, the level of foreign trade, per capita, is higher in Switzerland than in any other industrial nation. Per capita annual trade in Switzerland is valued at $15,035. In second place is Germany, at $8,132 per person. By comparison, the per capita trade figure is just $2,953 in the United States and $3,141 in Japan -- which are the world's two biggest trading giants in terms of total volume of trade.

The keys to Swiss success are found in the basic characteristics of its people. Their virtues, now beginning to return to favor in much of the rest of the world, include conservatism, individual freedom, self-sufficiently, thrift and a healthy skepticism of central government.

Labor-Management Co-operation

The "Protestant Work Ethic" was developed by a Swiss teacher and preacher, John Calvin, who set up a model church in Geneva in the 16th Century. Calvin turned Geneva into the "Rome" of the Protestant world, laying down a code of hard work, including the value of "saving for a rainy day" -- traits which have defined the Swiss character for the last 500 years or so and have an especially important outlet in the Swiss banking and insurance systems.

The Swiss are a nation of hard-working, somewhat quiet citizens -- the kind of responsible people you would want living next door to you -- or holding your money in trust for you. Swiss folk are hard-working, even strict, severe and disciplined. But that doesn't mean the Swiss are without humor, intelligence, imagination or depth. Switzerland has served as intellectual crossroads of all important European currents of thought for over 500 years, for instance:

The Swiss-born Jean-Jacques Rousseau, for instance, was the intellectual father of the American Revolution, exporting Swiss-style democratic ideas to the world, including the virtue of small units of government, built through a social contract between the people and their local government.

More great books have been written in Switzerland (because of its lack of censorship codes) than any nation in Europe. It has been the nation of great literary "exiles" for over 300 years, for authors ranging from Voltaire to Lenin.

As for science, Zurich's Federal Institute of Technology has produced more Nobel Prize winners than any other scientific school in the world. The great Swiss analytical psychologist, Carl Jung, among many others, taught there.

Part of the Swiss work ethic is a result of their chronic scarcity of natural resources. The Swiss have to be careful with what they own. They can't afford to waste any time, resources or money. Swiss houses, for instance, are built with exquisite care, to last for several generations, even centuries.

One observer said the Swiss combine the best of the Germanic love of order and thoroughness with a Latin independence of spirit and an admiration for quality and craftsmanship. Whether or not these traits are ethnic in origin, these qualities are definitely ingrained into the Swiss character today.

Swiss quality of manufacturing is respected worldwide, in watches and optics, for instance. (Craftsmanship is essential in a land which can waste no resources.) One result of this work ethic is that the Swiss have the highest levels of savings relative to GNP of any nation in the world -- about $15,000 per person -- and they work more hours every week -- 42.5 hours on average, compared to 37 hours for all of Europe. That work ethic results in unusual harmony between labor and management.

In 1973, for instance, all metal workers renounced the use of strikes as a tool of labor negotiations, and most other industries followed. In Switzerland, labor unrest is almost unheard of, because management rewards their workers well and keeps them informed on the financial details of the company. As a bonus, workers are usually paid a 13th month of salary at the end of each year.

Furthermore, most trades and crafts use apprentices instead of unions to renew their resources of labors. As a result, job-hopping is unusual in Switzerland and strikes are virtually unknown. There hasn't been a single industrial strike in Switzerland in the past 50 years. While Americans lose two hours per person per year to strikes, and all of the OECD (developed nations) lose an average of five hours per person per year, the Swiss have lost far less than one minute per person per year to strikes!

Because of a happy, efficient, well-rewarded working class, Switzerland has the lowest unemployment figures in the world, averaging 0.7% for the decade of the 1980s, sometimes sinking to as low as 0.1%. It also has the lowest poverty or crime rate of any major nation. The people you meet in Switzerland are uniformly polite, conservative and efficient.

Monetary Responsibility

From an investment perspective, the most important key to superior Swiss performance over the decades has been the strong Swiss currency. The Swiss franc is quite simply the world's best-managed currency. From a base value of just 23-cents in 1971 -- when most of the world's currencies were set free from the gold standard and began floating against each other -- the Swiss franc has grown stronger than any other currency in the world. Here are the essential facts:

An investment of just $2,300 in 1971 would have bought 10,000 Swiss francs. By 1978, those same 10,000 Swiss francs (even discounting interest income over 7 years) were worth $6,950 -- or three times their 1971 value.

Once again, in the mid-1980s, a U.S. investor could have purchased 10,000 Swiss francs for just $3,875, and then watched them double in value, to $7,800, in less than three years, and up to $8,000 by 1990 (not counting interest).

No other currency -- including the widely-heralded Japanese yen and German mark -- come close to the total performance of the Swiss franc. Even though Japan and Germany are mighty industrial powers, they have not managed their currencies nearly as well, or as consistently, as the Swiss. Japan has engaged in speculative excess in its financial markets, while Germany has taken on the costly task of supporting East Germany's emergence from its communist Dark Age -- to the point of backing the nearly-worthless East German mark with the same financial promises as the more solid West German mark.

Although past performance is no guarantee for the future, the Swiss franc should continue to post equally striking gains against all other currencies in the years ahead. The same reasons for its strong performance in the past remain in effect today, because they lie deep in the nature of Switzerland and the Swiss. They are based on political stability, safety and fiscal conservatism.

The Swiss Franc -- World's Safest Currency

The Swiss franc's superior performance is no accident. Swiss political, social and economic stability have helped the franc outperform all other currencies, not just since 1971, but since the 1920s and before. There are many sound reasons behind the strength of the Swiss franc, and they all come back to superior Swiss-style money management:

(1) **Gold Backing**. On April 18, 1999, Swiss voters gave their qualified approval to a new constitution which contains a provision effectively ending the statutory gold backing of the Swiss franc. Under the old constitution, every Swiss franc in circulation had to be backed by 40% in gold reserves. Using the artificial price of Sfr. 4,596 per kilogram as mandated by that Constitution, Switzerland's gold reserves of some Sfr. 12 billion were just more than enough to cover the statutory level at 43%. Applying current market prices, however, gold reserves of Sfr. 43 bn significantly exceed currency in circulation at about 130%.

In the new constitution, specifically Article 99, paragraph 3, it merely states that the Swiss National Bank accumulates reserves, a portion of which shall be in gold. With the independence of the SNB now also newly guaranteed in the constitution (paragraph 2 of Art. 99), the SNB can choose what portion of reserves to hold in gold. A specific level of gold relative to the currency is no longer mandated. Swiss monetary authorities are acutely aware of the need to maintain confidence in the Swiss franc, and the psychological support, if nothing else, gold-backing lends. In a speech by Dr. Peter Klauser of the Swiss National Bank to an academic audience, he concluded that "gold in the long-term rises in value in relation to the loss of purchasing power of a central bank's currency." It has also been acknowledged that gold as the only government-independent medium of payment is essential in preserving Swiss neutrality. From this perspective, gold will likely continue to play a crucial role in the Swiss central bank's portfolio.

(2) **No Exchange Controls**. Switzerland is the only country in the Eastern hemisphere which has never imposed external exchange controls on the outflow of funds. The knowledge that one's money will never be held hostage make more investors buy that currency, thus bidding its price up.

(3) **Political Neutrality**. Switzerland maintains strict neutrality. In times of war and political unrest, this neutrality protects the wealth of all peoples, of any political affiliation, until peace is restored.

(4) **Strong Democracy, Weak Government**. The Swiss control their government -- not the other way around -- through the national referendum and initiatives. Switzerland is the world's oldest and purest democracy.

(5) **Frugal Traditions**. The Swiss enjoy the highest per capita wealth and income in the Western world, with a long-established tradition of financial privacy and fiscal responsibility.

(6) **Low Money Growth**. Swiss money supply growth is low and stable, which is the best indicator that the Swiss franc will enjoy low inflation rates over a long-term scenario, maintaining its strong purchasing power in the future.

National Defense

Switzerland is like an entire nation of militia men. Half a million trained Swiss warriors are ready to fight at any moment's notice, but they will likely never need to use their world-class fighting skills against an invader.

When Hitler wanted to invade Switzerland in 1939, his generals told him that if he made such a foolish move, he would lose the war right there. Instead, Nazi troops went around Switzerland, to invade Austria and other countries. The value of conquering the Swiss was not worth the price it would have taken. It takes a tough army to allow a neutral nation to stay neutral this long.

Switzerland has armed sentries at all border crossings, with 3,000 points of demolition on bridges and tunnels. Most of this defense structure is totally invisible by air. Hewn into the mountainsides are arsenals, hospitals, and even fighter plane hangars, with the highways built to serve as emergency runways. An entire army division can fit inside some hidden mountain holes that otherwise appear as unsullied as a picture postcard. There is no part of picturesque Switzerland that is not ready to erupt into battle to repel invading armies.

Many Swiss bomb shelters even contain fully equipped hospitals and food for a year. Underground cities are stocked with stores of gold and currency for the post-war reconstruction phase. While other nations provide such bunkers only for their political and military leaders, the Swiss provide this protection for all.

There are over 600,000 assault rifles in Swiss homes, one for every ten people, or one for every five males. There are thousands of rounds of ammunition in sealed boxes in each home, and a prohibition against breaking the seal in peace time.

Military experts estimate that if this 650,000-man civilian army were warned in the morning, they would be mobilized by noon. The Swiss army is the largest in Europe, well-equipped, permanently trained, and yet the Swiss government only spends 1.9% of the GNP on defense. The rest is volunteer effort.

The private sector makes the Swiss defense system work, by paying each male citizen his full salary while he serves in the military two or three weeks a year between the ages of 20 and 50. Many others -- such as women, men over 50 and the disabled -- serve in the Civil National Defense Service.

Defense is a co-operative community effort, rather than the traditional division between military and civilian roles. For instance, the Swiss are the only soldiers in the world who keep their equipment, arms and ammunition at home and perform their obligatory gunnery duty each year in civilian clothes, showing the unusually high level of unity between civilian and military interests.

Summary: Why Invest In Switzerland?

Here are some of the political, economic and investment reasons to consider Switzerland and the Swiss franc for geographical and currency diversification:

1 No exchange controls have ever been placed on the outflow of money from Switzerland.

2 Swiss political neutrality in times of war and global unrest protect you from political theft of your wealth.

3 The Swiss people hold power over their federal government through the process of the referendum and initiative.

4 Gold reserves amount to at least twice the volume of Swiss franc currency in circulation.

5 High per capita wealth and financial responsibility reflect the Swiss work ethic and carry over to respect for your money.

6 Stable money supply indicates historically low inflation and strong purchasing power for the Swiss franc in the future.

7 Switzerland is the oldest democracy in the world -- now over 700 years old -- and certainly won't change its nature overnight.

The Bottom Line -- Switzerland is Still #1

Here are two independent rating services that listed Switzerland #1 for financial and political safety in 1991, taking all conceivable risks into account:

(1) **The Risk Ratings**: Switzerland is the safest country (out of 129), according to the International Country Risk Guide, counting political risk, financial risk and composite risk, 100 being total safety. Any score above 85 is considered "very low risk." The top 10 as of a recent edition are:

1. Switzerland	91.5	6. Netherlands	86.0
2. Luxembourg	89.0	7. Brunei	85.5
3. Norway	88.0	8. Japan	84.5
4. Austria	87.5	9. Singapore	83.5
5. Germany	86.0	10. USA	83.5

(2) **Institutional Investor** magazine rates the top 10 countries (for investor safety and services, in a recent issue) in the following order:

1. Switzerland	93.2	6. USA	87.2
2. Japan	92.5	7. Great Britain	84.6
3. Germany	90.6	8. Austria	84.3
4. Holland	87.8	9. Canada	83.7
5. France	87.4	10. Belgium	79.9

Chapter Two

The U.S. vs. Switzerland -- A Tale of Two Philosophies

"Throughout history, one of the ways that empires have collapsed -- Spain, Holland, Britain, for example -- is through debt. There came a point in Britain, after World War II, in which the debt became something the country couldn't deal with, so it was no longer a political issue. We have reached that point in {the U.S.} now."

-- Kevin Phillips, U.S. Political Commentator

In this chapter, we'll compare the U.S. economy, its financial institutions and currency, to the financial safety, performance, flexibility and privacy available with the same types of investments in Switzerland. As you will see, it's a story of quantity vs. quality, of size vs. stability.

Debt Threatens to Cripple the U.S. Economy

The level of debt in the U.S. economy -- from the federal government through state governments, corporations and individuals -- is almost beyond counting: It's now measured in trillions of dollars at each level. None of us fully understand what a trillion means, but the per capita debt is more imaginable -- you (and each member of your family) owe $14,000 per person on the federal deficit alone, and you owe more than $50,000 (per person) counting all levels of debt. Here are just a few examples of how debt has risen astronomically in just the last decade, from a level that Americans once thought was intolerable (i.e., under Carter in 1980).

I. Government Debt

The federal deficit was less than $1 trillion when Ronald Reagan was sworn into office in 1981, but it is over $3.5 trillion now, and is growing at a rate of more than 10% ($350 billion) per year.

State government deficits are now growing at even a faster rate than the federal government (and they don't have the power to print money to finance those debts). Seven states now have multi-billion-dollar-per-year deficits.

The ratio of private and public debt to GNP is now 50% higher than it was in 1980, and is nearing record levels set in the deepest Depression year, 1932.

II. Personal Debt

Household debt (mortgage, auto and installment debt) has now reached an astronomical 85% of disposable (after tax) income, up from 59% in 1983.

Family outlays (bills paid) for consumer debt (not including mortgage debt) have risen from 14% of each paycheck in 1983 to 19% in 1990.

Household disposable income, after taxes, debts and essentials, is now below 4%, down from 12% in 1983.

Personal bankruptcy filings have increased from less than 200,000 per year in any year before 1980, to over 850,000 now.

Credit card debt rose from $54.9 billion in 1980 to $215.8 billion in 1990.

Car loans rose from $111.9 billion in 1980 to $285.2 billion in 1990.

II. Corporate debt

Corporate bankruptcies have gone up from a range of 10,000 to 15,000 per year, from 1950 to 1980, skyrocketing to 80,000 in 1991.

Corporate long-term debt, due in the next five years, has gone from $508 billion in 1986 to $864 billion (up 70% in five years). As a percentage of net worth, long term debt has risen from 19% to 31%.

Bond defaults totalled only about one billion dollars in 1982, despite a deep recession and all-time high interest rates (including a 21% Prime Rate). But bond defaults have doubled each of the last three years: $5 billion in 1988, $12 billion in 1989, $25 billion in 1990 and $50 billion in 1991.

Debt inside the U.S. banking system has increased 6-fold in the past 20 years, leading to several bank failures, while financial debt **outside** the banks -- mostly in S&Ls and insurance companies -- has grown about nine times over the same period.

One in five S&Ls has already failed, while another one in five is technically insolvent or below minimum capital requirements.

Six of the ten largest U.S. insurance companies have high risk assets equal to, or exceeding, 100% of their total surplus capital.

The U.S. Dollar's Growing Problems

The U.S. has run tremendous trade deficits over the last decade, exporting hundreds of billions of increasingly worthless dollars in exchange for imported consumer goods. America has had lower inflation in the 1980s, partly due to this large **export of dollars** overseas. The result: There are fewer dollars in America, chasing less of your domestic wealth. But when the trade deficit finally turns around (that is, when the dollar is recognized as being weaker than the currencies of most of America's trading partners), the process will go into reverse and the U.S. will be flooded with weak dollars.

The dollar has gone through several distinct cycles in the 20 years since it (and other major currencies) were set free to "float" according to market demand, when Nixon closed the gold window on August 15, 1971. The cycles have led to higher highs and higher "lows" for the Swiss franc, compared with lower highs and lower lows for the U.S. dollar. In the 1970s, many savvy investors tripled their money on the Swiss franc -- not counting interest rate yields -- as the Swiss franc rose from about 23 cents in 1971, to 69 cents in 1978.

Then, in the early 1980s, the Swiss franc declined almost 50%. For five years, the Swiss franc drifted lower, to under 39 cents to the dollar. By the end of 1987 -- less than three years later -- the Swiss franc doubled in value to 78 cents. Once again, this does not count the interest you would have accrued on a Swiss franc investment. After a brief respite, the Swiss franc again leaped up to 80 cents in 1990.

Each succeeding "low" in the cycle is higher than the previous low, while each new "high" takes the Swiss franc higher, on its way to parity (and beyond) with the U.S. dollar. Taking all the ups and downs of the last two decades into consideration, the Swiss franc is still the best performing currency of all, and the one most reliable currency for the future. Here's a rundown of the three strongest currencies since they were set afloat in 1971:

Hard Currencies **To the US Dollar**	**Starting** **In 1971**	**Peaking** **in 1990**	**Percent** **Growth**
Swiss franc	$0.2325	$0.800	244%
Japanese Yen	$0.0028	$0.008	186%
German mark	$0.2500	$0.680	172%

Except for these three, **no other currencies come close** to holding their value for the two decades since 1971. This level of performance is no accident. Switzerland's political, social and economic stability have earned this level of performance. Long term, the Swiss franc has performed better than any currency in the world, since 1914, since 1926, since 1940, since 1971 and since 1985. Almost any long-term time frame finds the Swiss franc out in front.

Since 1926, when the franc became completely independent as a world currency, it has not lost value against any major currency for more than a very few years at a time. While other currencies have virtually disappeared during or after a great war, the Swiss franc keeps gaining comparative value.

Just comparing the U.S. dollar to the Swiss franc, look what happened to the value of $10,000 in each of the two currencies over the last 20 years (discounting interest income). The first column takes inflation into account, dramatizing the drop in purchasing power of the dollar, while the right hand column shows the changing value of $10,000 in current terms, including inflation (but not interest):

Year	Amount in Constant 1970 U.S. Dollars	Amount in current dollars if held in Swiss francs
1970	$10,000	$10,000
1975	$6,700	$14,600
1980	$3,000	$25,800
1990	$1,800	$34,400

Swiss Inflation Is Historically Low

Switzerland has traditionally been one of the most anti-inflationary nations in the world. Swiss inflation rates have varied from zero to 6% over the last 20 years, averaging barely 2%. When the U.S. had double-digit inflation in 1975, for instance, the Swiss inflation rate was among the lowest in the world, 1.7%. When President Ford "whipped inflation now" back in 1977, the Swiss brought their inflation rate down to 0.5% while the U.S. inflation rate stayed above 6% for nearly a decade. Switzerland's average inflation for the 1970s was 2.3%.

In 1991, however, Swiss inflation reached an unusually high 5.8%, following 5.4% growth in consumer prices in 1990. The Swiss have seldom seen inflation rates at such a high level, and so the Swiss Central Bank is taking the right steps to bring inflation rates back under 2% to 3% in 1992 and beyond.

High inflation in 1990 and 1991 resulted from an unfortunate decision in 1987 and 1988, to add more money to an already fully employed economy. M1 money supply grew by an un-Swiss-like rate of 13.7% in 1987. Since price inflation usually follows monetary inflation after a two-year lag, prices began to shoot up in 1989. However, the Swiss central bank started a very tight monetary policy in late 1989 -- money supply actually fell by 6% in 1989 and 1990 (see table, next page) -- so price inflation should start falling to typically low Swiss figures by late 1992.

Except for the unusually high money supply growth rate in 1987 (see table, next page), the money supply in Switzerland usually stays level or declines from year to year. In several recent years, Swiss money supply actually declined, and the net growth has been very small, 1.4%. Consider the most recent six-year period:

Swiss Money Supply (M1)

At year-end, billions of SFr.

	Year-end M-1 Money supply	Gain (or loss) In previous year
1984	75.91	N/A
1985	73.94	(2.6%)
1986	75.49	2.1%
1987	85.87	13.7%*
1988	87.81	2.3%
1989	85.56	(2.6%)
1990	82.54	(3.5%)
Total 6-year Growth (1984-90)		+8.7%
Average growth, per year:		+1.4%

***Note** the 13.7% money supply growth in 1987. That is the main cause of the high (5%-6%) Swiss price inflation in 1990-91. However, the decline in money supply in 1989 and 1990 (down about 3% each year), should lower price inflation in 1992-93.

Compared to the ballooning U.S. budget deficits of the 1980s, the Swiss have had a budget surplus every fiscal year since 1986. In fact, the 1988 Swiss budget surplus of $800 million would equate to a $32 billion surplus in the U.S. By contrast, the U.S. government went $160 further into debt in fiscal year 1988, and that was the **lowest** deficit for the late 1980s. U.S. red ink doubled that level, to more than $330 billion, in the latest (1991) budget deficit.

Swiss Budget Revenues and Outlays, 1984-1989 (in billions of Swiss francs)

Revenues	Outlays	Surplus (or deficit)	
1984	19.98	20.55	(0.57)
1985	20.78	20.88	(0.10)
1986	24.02	21.72	+2.30
1987	23.45	21.56	+1.89
1988	28.11	24.42	+3.69
1989	25.60	26.34	(0.74)
Totals	141.94	135.47	+6.47

In this recent six-year period in which the U.S. budget deficits exceeded $1.2 trillion, the Swiss managed to turn a budget surplus in three straight years and ended the period with a 6.4 billion Swiss franc net budget **surplus.**

This comparison in fiscal management will result in increasing sickness for the U.S. dollar. Budget deficits of $300 billion a year, a public debt quickly rising from $3 to $4 trillion, sick banks, Savings & Loans and giant insurance companies, a loss of any semblance of gold backing, and a long-term (since 1982) 8% annual increase in money supply combine to make any careful investor suspicious of placing all his wealth in such a sick currency.

Meanwhile, the strength of the Swiss franc is liable to continue as long as the Swiss money managers act responsibly and the U.S. managers do not.

Purchasing Power Parity (PPP) Measures Swiss Superiority

Why currencies rise and fall over the short-term can be mystifying. Watching the currency markets day to day can be baffling. These daily fluctuations of value are a subject of theoretical controversy among experts, but over the long term, the reasons for strength or weakness is more clear. Major, freely-traded currencies are valued according to their Purchasing Power Parity (PPP), which means that the price of a currency will drop in relation to another currency when -- over a long period of time -- its level of inflation is higher than the other.

To find the best currencies (and worst) in the world, look at the three economic indicators that are most in control of the central bank, or any other government institution: (1) the level of new money supply, (2) the level of government spending and deficits, and (3) the inflation (and interest) rate. The higher these figures are, the worse the condition the currency will be in. The lower these numbers are, the better value the currency is for the long term.

Holding all your funds at all times in any one currency, even the Swiss franc, is needlessly risky. But due to the superior money management of the Swiss National Bank, sooner or later the Swiss franc will continue to rise against the U.S. dollar, to perhaps a parity level of one U.S. dollar to one Swiss franc.

Erosion of Financial Privacy in the U.S.

Perhaps you've noticed that in the United States, your financial life has become almost totally transparent to the government, private credit agencies and an army of shady salesmen. For instance, notice how often you are asked for personal financial information -- your salary or income level, the balance on your loans, or your Social Security Number (SSN), which is the key that unlocks all your files. Even if you don't volunteer this information, your SSN reveals your income, deductions, deposits, investments and even more private information to whomever can access such files. At the minimum, the IRS has all your tax filings on magnetic tape, and private credit agencies (such as Equifax or TRW) contain all the information you put on a loan application or medical insurance form.

Even though you supplied most of that information yourself -- so you assume it's at least accurate -- that's not usually the case. Private credit agencies also ask your neighbors and business associates probing questions about you for their files. Who knows what kind of misconceptions people spread about you, or what kind of mistaken transcriptions are on your file? The horror stories abound.

To fight back, you can begin giving out less information on yourself. Start by not filling in every blank line you see on a form. Put N/A (not applicable, or not available) on lines that seem too probing. You can also use more non-traceable types of cash instruments more often -- like money orders, cashier's checks or traveller's checks -- rather than personal checks (which are all microfilmed for the IRS at your bank) or credit cards, which chronicle your spending habits.

Even if you are as careful as possible, there's only so much you can do to maintain financial privacy in the U.S. The IRS will demand a certain level of disclosure, if you want to take any deductions at all. A better solution is to have at least a portion of your wealth in a safe haven where no prying eyes can attach, sue, tax, or steal them. You'll also cut down on sales calls putting pressure on you to buy some new investment you don't really want to hear about.

Please understand: Financial privacy has nothing to do with breaking laws or evading taxes. But it has everything to do with protecting your duly-earned, tax-deferred, tax-sheltered, or after-tax wealth that deserves a safe home.

You can't go just anywhere overseas to gain privacy. Some tiny Caribbean islands may claim Swiss-style privacy, but they don't have the 250-year tradition and solid AAA-rated banks and insurance companies that are the norm in Switzerland. If you took the time to examine every country on earth to find the safest haven, you would find that all roads lead to Switzerland as the best second home for your assets.

Some Current Laws Restricting Financial Freedom in America

You may feel completely comfortable sacrificing your financial privacy to today's government in the U.S., but you never know what tomorrow's politicians might dream up. Best-selling author Doug Casey has put it bluntly: "One of the fixed points in the cosmos is the stupidity and malevolence of government."

It would be impossible to list all the invasions of privacy that assault a typical American investor in one year, but here are just a few of the latest intrusions the government has invented. One governmental idea is to require U.S. citizens to file a "Cash Transaction Report" (CTR) for any transaction above $10,000. The idea was to catch drug dealers laundering money, but international drug dealers are too smart to get caught in this trap. Instead, it catches the moderately successful investor.

For instance, if you're involved in real estate financing, you will likely be involved with several five-figure transactions each year. This is also true if you trade or switch investment funds often. You must fill out a CRT each time. This seemingly "harmless" form puts you on the same list as international drug dealers and suspected money launderers.

Another malevolent idea in the U.S. is to encode all newly printed dollar bills with a black magnetic filament designed to trip the metal detectors at America's borders and allow the customs officers to grab anyone trying to "smuggle" their money out of the country. Putting cash in the same category as sub-machine guns is an idea that only a government can conceive!

U.S. laws also require that a banker make all bank records accessible to the IRS, and other government agencies on demand. By comparison, Swiss law makes such bank co-operation a crime. Even the Swiss government, much less the IRS, can't penetrate a Swiss bank account unless a Swiss court order is obtained, and such a court order cannot be issued unless the Swiss government clearly shows that a Swiss crime has likely been committed and the information in the bank account is necessary to the prosecution of the case.

All the current and future laws restricting your free transport of capital must make any concerned American investor anxious. If there is a significant risk that U.S. borders will be closed to the departure of wealth some day, isn't now the time to get some of it out, before the penalties are raised to the danger point? In the best of all possible worlds, the threat never materializes and you are still earning good returns on your money in a safer country and a more secure currency. The knowledge that a portion of your wealth is waiting for you, where nobody can touch it but you, creates a sense of security and freedom from fear. That's a level of security you can't put a price on.

Tax evasion -- which is a crime in the U.S. -- is only a civil (not criminal) offense in Switzerland. That means the U.S. government cannot go to the Swiss government on suspected U.S. tax evasion charges and penetrate the account of a U.S. citizen. Nor can the U.S. government obtain information on your Swiss financial account if you break laws regarding the mere holding of, or reporting of, a foreign bank account. Under Swiss law, it is not a crime (or a civil offense) to hold a foreign bank account, or transport funds across national borders. In fact, such freedom of capital movement is the norm in Europe, rather than the exception.

Chapter Three

Why You Need the Safety of Swiss Diversification

"Never keep all your wealth in the country where you live. Keep part of your assets hidden. Only then will you know that you own something somewhere that the government isn't going to get its hands on."

-- *Harry Browne*

The case for diversification is clear. Nobody is safe if they put 100% of their assets into real estate, or growth stocks, or a single currency or bank CD. Your performance is severely hampered if you ignore all of the investment options that are available in the rest of the world. Most importantly, U.S. investors need to be aware of the severe threats to their wealth, if all of it is held in the U.S.

American investors face two major monetary hurdles in the 1990s: (1) making money that is not eroded by government-caused inflation, or lost or stolen in unpredictable and dangerous investment markets; then (2) keeping that money from being taxed into oblivion. As U.S. economic conditions continue to deteriorate in the 1990s, and government intervention in American investors' personal lives escalates, many Americans have reached the conclusion that they should get part or all of their wealth out of the U.S., while it is still legal to do so.

There are basically three major types of diversification:

- By type of investment -- stocks, bonds, cash, real estate, gold, etc.
- By Currency -- U.S. dollar, Swiss franc, German mark, etc.
- By Geographical location of your financial account

How to diversify? The successful international investment manager John Templeton has **three basic common-sense principles:**

(1) Look for opportunities in areas where socialism is the weakest. The greater the tendency in any country toward the expropriation of private wealth, the greater the chance that your wealth will be undermined. Socialism is currently weakest in nations like Hong Kong in Asia and Switzerland in Europe.

(2) For stock market investing, look for industries that are the least prone to government regulation. Stay away from state-controlled industries.

(3) Look for nations where inflation is likely to remain low. High inflation disrupts business and investment markets. Investing gives way to speculation. Consistently low inflation rates make for predictable profits.

A major drawback to overseas investing in **most** nations has been the specter of exchange controls. Most European nations have slapped on exchange controls whenever they sense a currency crisis looming. France, Germany, and even England have instituted exchange controls in this century. The Swiss, of course, have never instituted controls on funds leaving their country. The only controls have been brief limitations on how much money one can bring **into** Switzerland.

Having some assets in another country makes good sense. By investing abroad, you can watch events at home in the secure knowledge that at least some of your property is beyond the reach of future confiscation or forced disclosure.

Why invest in a foreign country? All other things being equal, you probably should not. You know your own country much better than any other country. Everyone speaks your language at home. The currency is familiar to you. Your money is physically closer to you, and you might feel more comfortable keeping your money close to your vest, in case of emergency.

But all things are not equal. Some currencies perform consistently better than others. For instance, the

U.S. dollar performs consistently better than the Mexican peso, and the peso excels the Nicaraguan cordoba or Brazilian cruzeiro.

Financial Institutions in the U.S. May No Longer Be Safe

Banks and other financial institutions are clearly not safe in the U.S. anymore. The number of bank failures have set new postwar records every year in the 1980s, peaking with 224 bank failures in the supposedly "prosperous" year of 1989. If bank failures are rising this fast during an unprecedented period of prosperity, think how much faster they will rise toward the end of this severe "double-dip" recession.

With the FDIC "insurance" dwindling from $20 billion in 1983, to less than $2 billion today, the widely hailed government "insurance" will soon become another taxpayer bailout. Your $100,000 account insurance, far from being your savior in hard times, helped cause this problem. Investors who relied on this insurance had no incentive to deposit their money in a traditionally "safe" bank. After all, the government would bail them out. So they went for the highest possible yield, regardless of the bank's safety.

The same lack of prudent judgment ruled the bank's investment committee. They went for the highest yielding junk bonds as "assets," since the government would obviously bail out any mistakes. But the government never bails out bank mismanagement, the taxpayers do.

Compare the health of U.S. banks to Swiss banks. While a bank in the U.S. might have only 4% to 5% capital, relative to total assets to offset problem loans, Swiss banks often have capital equal to 20% or more of assets, and they have little (if any) problem loans to offset.

Additionally, the assets of a Swiss bank are likely to be more truthfully stated than those of American banks. For example, a Swiss bank, by law, must carry its bond holdings at market value on its statement of condition, while American banks carry them at original cost. (When interest rates rise, as they will likely do soon, the market value of bonds becomes substantially less than the original cost.)

S&Ls and Insurance Companies Make U.S. Banks Look Healthy

The good news about U.S. banks is that they are in better shape than any other major financial institution in America. As problematic as the banks in the U.S. may be, the U.S. Savings and Loans (S&Ls) are worse, and insurance companies are becoming worse still. The S&Ls have been technically insolvent since 1986, with a net value of minus $6 billion in 1986, minus $13.7 billion in 1987, minus $20 billion in 1988 and minus nearly $50 billion in

1991. The Congressional bill to rescue the S&Ls started with a price tag of $164 billion in 1989, but quickly escalated beyond $500 billion by now, or about $2,000 for each American citizen.

And now we see the emerging collapse of the insurance industry in the U.S., perhaps representing a greater total loss than the banks and S&Ls combined. The percentage of sick or underfunded insurers is even greater than the percentage of sick S&Ls -- and insurance companies have a larger capital base.

The problem started in the 1980s, when insurance companies vied with each other to offer annuities and other long-term investments with a higher rate of return than their competitors. To get these returns, insurance companies invested in something that they would have shunned just a decade earlier -- "junk bonds." What's more, the mutual insurance industry is not subject to the public disclosure requirements of banks and S&Ls, and so the percentage of junk bonds in most insurance companies was severely under-reported until recently, when S&P bond rating standards were finally adopted.

When junk bonds began to fail **en masse** in late 1989 and early 1990, the secret was out of the bag. Many (in fact more than 50% in most cases) of the bonds which had been carried on insurance books as "investment grade" were found to be middle-grade "junk" by the widely accepted ratings of Standard & Poor's.

Perhaps your insurance agent sold you an annuity or insurance policy based on the widely quoted A.M. Best ratings. Best is the insurance industry's in-house rating system and is overly generous. A.M. Best lists most large companies as "A" or "A+" for safety, at the same time that several major insurance companies have failed to qualify for the top two grades of S&P or Moody's and, in fact, have been downgraded by those respected ratings services lately.

By investing in Switzerland, you also profit from the advice and guidance of investment professionals steeped in the timeless Swiss principles of safe, private, consistent wealth building. This will come as a dramatic and refreshing change from what you may be accustomed to, when dealing with U.S. bankers or brokers.

Take a moment to look at some of these basic Swiss investment principles.

Swiss Investment Principles

The Swiss grow up believing, and being taught, that every person's investment portfolio should start with a solid base, like the base of a pyramid, in low risk investments. This is followed by a smaller, mid-section of the pyramid containing balanced growth investments, with a small amount of prudent speculations on top. The basic idea of using the pyramid is to give an investor a proper perspective on every investment decision he makes. The pyramid should ideally be bottom-heavy:

BASE	60%	in conservative, long-term investments
MIDDLE	30%	in normal-risk, cyclical investments
TOP	10%	in higher-risk, speculative investments

The expected yield from each these sectors looks just the opposite. For the bottom 60%, the price for low risk is a real annual yield in the range of 5% over the long-term. For the middle section, real yields can range from 10% to 20%, but those yields are not guaranteed. For the top portion, you may expect 25% or more in yields, but only if you guess right. Put all these sectors together and your ideal gains will be around 10% per year, if everything works according to plan:

I. A model $100,000 portfolio, when everything goes as planned:

$60,000 x 1.05 (60% @ 5% gains) = $63,000

$30,000 x 1.15 (30% @ 15% gains) = $34,500

$10,000 x 1.25 (10% @ 25% gains) = <u>$12,500</u>

TOTAL YIELD = 1.10 (10% per year) = $110,000 (+10%)

However, if you make a disastrous decision in the top, speculative portion of your pyramid -- and its value goes **down** 30% -- and you make a second mistake by choosing growth investments that don't grow at all, you still keep liquid and retain your net worth because of your solid base. Even though the tip of your pyramid is chipped off, your total investment portfolio survives unscathed:

II. A model $100,000 when everything goes "badly":

$60,000 x 1.05(60% @ 5% gains)		=	$63,000
$30,000 x 1.00(30% @ zero gain)		=	$30,000
$10,000 x 0.70(10% @ 30% loss)		=	$7,000
TOTAL YIELD =	None	=	100,000 (no gain or loss)

Analyzing Each Level of the Pyramid

The percentage you choose to place in each portion of your portfolio may vary, depending on your age, wealth and investment goals, but it is important that you recognize and separate all of your investments into these three sections.

(1) **The base of your pyramid** is your top priority, helping to insure your financial security for life, through long-term solid investments. These include annuities, gold accumulation and conservative securities. The base of the pyramid always has to be large enough to support the risks taken at the top. In fact, having a sound

and secure asset foundation is what enables an investor to take intelligent risks without jeopardizing his financial future. These base investments should hold their value in both good and bad times, and in either moderate inflation or deflation.

In the base of the pyramid, the only criterion you're concerned with is the return **of** your assets, not the return **on** your assets. You're not chasing a profit-oriented yield in the base. These assets, regardless of what happens in the rest of the world, should ensure your living expenses and essentials. Therefore, the base portion should include a reasonable percentage of physical gold, real estate, endowments and deferred annuities, insurance and conservative, carefully selected securities. The base could also include your tangible assets (cars, jewelry, antiques, land), your basic savings and checking accounts, corporate pension funds, life insurance value at maturity, prospective inheritance and value of your business (if you have one).

(2) **The growth portion**, in the middle, is designed to provide you with enough income to match the expected growth in your standard of living as you mature. You engineer this growth through making well-timed entries and exits in the cyclical investments, especially precious metals and stocks.

Cyclical investments benefit from the fact that the world's economies vacillate between growth and contraction. Many investments move in opposite directions at reasonably predictable cycles in the economy. In times of rising inflation, for instance, the emphasis is on tangible investments like gold; in times of falling inflation, bonds outperform most investments. The aim of these investments is to maintain purchasing power and receive a real return.

Remember, it is easier to make a profit in a second-class stock in a bull market than in a blue chip stock in a bear market. That's why timing is more important than selection of the stock when discussing most mutual funds, convertible bonds, gold shares, bonds, and currency time deposits.

(3) **The top portion** is speculative, with the goal of reaping a bonanza payoff in a fairly risky trading vehicle. This is the territory for options, futures, commodities, any riskier stocks and even riskier, high-yielding currencies. This top portion of the pyramid should be only a small percentage of your funds and is only advisable after the other two sectors are fully invested.

Whoever wishes to make a profit must risk a loss. There will never be a scientific method for speculating successfully or consistently. To make a profit, you must take risks. However, the point of your pyramid should be a **prudent** speculation. Avoid the "all or nothing" gambler's syndrome, which can cause your pyramid to prematurely lose its point!

Take time now -- if you haven't done so recently -- to examine your own personal portfolio pyramid. List your assets in each of these three categories -- the conservative, permanent base; cyclical growth investments (buy low, sell high); and your speculations. Then figure the percentage of your holdings in each category of the pyramid, and your total net worth -- which is the total value of all your capital, minus debts. If your investments are not sufficiently "bottom-heavy," then perhaps you should consider adjusting the ratio of the three segments. In some cases, a top-heavy (speculative) pyramid might just be appropriate to your age and goals.

The Typical Investor's Life Cycle

The percentages at each level of your portfolio depend on your age and net worth. The two main phases are the accumulation and consumption phases.

(1) **The accumulation phase** begins when an individual has completed his basic education and embarks on a trade, craft or profession. The investment goal of this phase of life is accumulation of wealth for future use, deferring some current gratification. Investments in this phase are selected for their appreciation potential. Within the accumulation phase, there are three sub-phases.

1. Subsistence phase (up to age 35)
2. Stabilization phase (ages 35 to 45)
3. Speculation phase (ages 45 to 60)

In the subsistence phase, you make provision for your income through continuing education. Typically, you will secure your health, accident and disability insurance. Your savings and life insurance value give you enough liquidity to maneuver in case of an emergency.

In the stabilization phase, you secure your living standard by entering into cyclical investments, in the middle of your investment pyramid. You profit from cycles in the markets by investing in mutual funds, stocks, gold and securities.

In the speculation phase, your life and income are usually more stabilized. Basic and fixed costs consume a smaller portion of your income, so you are free to take more risks, while you are still at your peak earning power. In case your speculations fail, you can earn more money to replace the top portion of your pyramid. This luxury will not be available once you retire.

Then comes retirement and the next major phase.

(2) **The consumption phase** begins at retirement (beginning some time after age 60 in most cases). This is the time to shift your capital into yields, so as to live from your life's earnings and begin to take life easier. You may invest in securities with a high yield, or buy an annuity in Swiss francs.

During this phase, you should plan on cashing in on your gold (gradually), and living on your fully paid real estate, if appropriate. At this time, most of your previously accumulated assets must be converted into income. Any new investments must be selected for their income-producing potential and security.

Your investment pyramid should become more base-heavy in these years, as in your early years. In rough terms, here is one way to balance consumption to accumulation, by investment type.

Accumulation Phase	Consumption Phase
Growth investments	Income investments
Real Estate	Income property
Gold accumulation	Turn gold into income
Savings accounts	Private pension plans
Deferred annuities	Income annuities

How Much Accumulation Is Enough?

The ideal retirement nest egg at the beginning of the harvest phase is about one million dollars, or even one million Swiss francs -- since the two currencies are likely to be equal in value sometime in the 1990s. Swiss bankers affectionately call a million Swiss francs a "chest." In English, you would likely call it a "nest egg."

Accumulating a million dollars, or a million Swiss francs, is not as difficult as it may sound. For instance, you can reach a million dollars by putting away just $5,000 per year at 7% interest for 40 years. In most cases, however, you won't have 40 years left to save. In such cases, you may need to save $10,000 or more per year -- or 10% of a $100,000 per year family income.

If you are currently behind on your accumulation phase, don't lose heart. It's never too late to start the savings habit. Set aside 10% of all income for long-term accumulation from this day forward. A full purse is always better than an empty one. Far from reducing your capabilities by limiting consumption, it opens up life's possibilities and brightens up your whole outlook on life. Far from being a boring Swiss habit, saving gives you aid in an emergency, can help you retire early, travel more, or take a job you like, instead of a job you need.

America has the lowest savings rate in the industrialized world. In America, over 40% of all consumer spending is financed, over 20% of corporate expenditures are debt service and over 15% of federal government expenditures are paid for with tomorrow's dollars through deficit spending. The United States is setting the worst possible financial example for the world.

Once you start saving 10% or more of your income, the magic of compound interest goes to work for you. Even at just 5% interest, and allowing for 35% taxation -- the worst numbers conceivable -- a savings accumulation plan of just $9,000 per year will become $252,444 after 20 years, $453,798 after 30 years and

$731,040 after a typical working life of 40 years. And that's assuming no capital appreciation, if the investment is held, partly or wholly, in Swiss francs. For a more likely set of assumptions -- higher interest, lower taxes, tax-deferred investments (such as a pension plan or annuity) and a favorable Swiss franc exchange rate over the next few decades -- you can probably double each of these figures.

Swiss Financial Planning For American Investors

Swiss-based institutions, with Swiss-based principles and investment options, make successful lifetime financial planning more of a reality than is possible in any other country. Swiss financial institutions meet the following four goals.

1) **Asset Preservation and Protection**. It's not uncommon for an American citizen to work hard for 40 or 50 years, accumulate a sizable nest egg, and then stand by and watch it destroyed through inflation, a falling currency, or failing investments. The preservation of a family's nest egg requires at least three safeguards: a safe currency, a safe financial institution, and political stability. The Swiss provide all three.

2) **Financial Freedom**. To most Americans, freedom is an important goal -- embedded in nearly all the nation's founding documents -- but perhaps the level of freedom in America doesn't have the vigor it once had,

some 200 years ago. Today, financial freedom comes from privacy and capital preservation which are present more perfectly in Switzerland than any nation on ear

3) **Tax Savings**. There are several fully legal ways to defer paying Swiss or U.S. taxes on Swiss-based investments. It is not your duty to pay the maximum amount of taxes possible. It is, in fact, your right to pay the least amount of taxes that is legally permissible. There are several well-accepted ways of avoiding both Swiss and U.S. taxes without breaking the spirit or the letter of the law.

4) **Responsibility**. Like the Swiss, many Americans have a firm sense of personal responsibility to take care of their own financial needs, and their family after they're gone, without asking for government handouts along the way. Despite all the hurdles thrown in front of such investors -- by a tax-hungry government, a sue-happy society, "get rich quick" advertising, and a consume-it-now society -- many Americans sincerely believe it is their duty to tend their nest egg responsibly, for tation. Investing in Switzerland is a major step toward meeting that goal.

Chapter Four

The Safest of the Safe: Swiss Banks & Insurance Companies

"Money is the seed of money, and the first guinea is sometimes more difficult to acquire than the second million."

-- Jean Jacques Rousseau (Swiss-born), from *"A Discourse on Political Economy"* (1758)

The first thing to understand about investing in Switzerland is that you have two choices -- Swiss banks or Swiss insurance companies. Unlike U.S. insurance companies, their Swiss counterparts offer a broad range of bank-like services. Many Swiss use their insurance company as their only financial institution.

Once you decide to send a portion of your wealth for safe deposit in Switzerland, you also have a choice among several types of investments. This chapter will briefly describe a typical Swiss investment menu, composed of Swiss franc savings accounts (in the form of annuities, Swiss insurance, gold held in Switzerland, Swiss-managed investment portfolios, and more.

But first, consider some of the tradeoffs between using Swiss banks and/or Swiss insurance companies to manage these investments for you.

Even though the world is enamored with the concept of having a "numbered Swiss bank account," the Swiss themselves use their bank account and insurance company interchangeably. Accounts with insurance companies in Switzerland offer what a bank or brokerage account would offer in America and much more.

Swiss Banks vs. Swiss Insurance Companies

Although the case for international diversification seems persuasive, it might also seem too unfamiliar for you to get started without more information. If that's the case, you can always consider opening a Swiss bank account with a small amount (say under $10,000, to avoid U.S. reporting requirements). Make it not only enough money to make sense for you and the bank, but also small enough that you'll begin to feel comfortable investing abroad.

Before long, you should discover that the Swiss are trustworthy professionals -- possibly even more so than your home town bankers. You'll enjoy the luxury of total privacy of your financial records, in contrast to your local bank, which keeps asking you to fill out government reporting forms, or sends information to the government without your permission.

At some point, you will be ready to use your small Swiss bank account to branch out into other Swiss investments, described in this book, which offer you more competitive returns, full Swiss safety, no reporting requirements, low (or no) taxes, and complete privacy from public and private snoops. (Making money is not enough these days; you must insure that you keep it as well.)

Swiss bank accounts are an excellent first step, for purposes of privacy and diversification. A Swiss bank account can often be a "home base" for selecting and managing other investments. Many Americans with quite modest savings goals use Swiss banks, and Swiss bankers usually welcome their deposits.

However, there are some drawbacks to maintaining a Swiss bank account:

- First, there is the obligation to disclose a Swiss bank account on your tax form. On Schedule B of your 1040 form, you are asked to check (yes or no) if you have had a foreign bank account any time during the year.
- Swiss bank accounts are no way to get rich; savings accounts usually pay only about 2.5% interest.
- Finally, there is that nagging Swiss withholding tax of 35% on your interest.

In short, there are many other Swiss investments which can be far more lucrative, private and versatile than bank accounts. In fact, many Swiss investment products are not "bank accounts" at all, and are therefore not required to be declared on your U.S. tax forms, or subject to Swiss withholding. These alternative Swiss investments include Swiss insurance accounts, managed investment accounts, annuities, gold accumulation accounts and more.

Super-Safe Swiss Insurance Companies

In Switzerland, insurance firms offer a greater range of financial services than most Swiss banks, along with the privacy and tax advantages mentioned earlier. There are far fewer Swiss insurance firms -- about 20 in all -- compared to thousands of insurers in the U.S. You literally cannot go wrong in selecting a Swiss insurance company. Unlike the U.S., there are no weak insurers in Switzerland.

A Swiss government body -- the Swiss Federal Bureau of Private Insurance (FOPI) -- strictly regulates the insurance agency, with the aim of protecting the depositor from overcharging or from under-performance. The Swiss watchdogs won't allow domestic insurance firms to hold high-yield or risky investments. The result is that there is virtually no difference in the rate of return between one Swiss insurance firm and another. The main difference is the amount of dividends paid, and competition between insurance firms keeps even that difference small.

The overseers at FOPI only approve insurance premiums which lie within the premium maximum (protection from overcharging) and minimum (guarantee of payment capability). The office makes sure the companies invest their funds as profitably as possible, in a broadly-based portfolio of investments to protect them against risk of overexposure to a single market. Every insurance company must meet strict Swiss standards for security, yield, diversification and liquidity.

No other sector of the Swiss economy is so rigorously supervised, nor does any other sector of the fiercely independent Swiss economy accept such a high level of federal supervision with such openness and co-operation -- especially since the insurance firms actually must pay the full cost of this supervision themselves.

In the U.S., every big insurance company has a rating from Moody's or Standard & Poor's, and nearly all U.S. insurance companies, small and large, are rated by A.M. Best. There are no comparable ratings services in Switzerland. But each of the Swiss firms would rate the equivalent of AAA by U.S. reporting standards.

Supervision of private insurance has existed as part of the Swiss Federal Constitution (Article 34, paragraph 2) for over s century, since 1885. FOPI restricts insurance companies to Swiss franc investments of the most conservative kind. As a result, no Swiss insurance company has ever closed its doors or failed to meet its obligations, much less filed for bankruptcy. In fact, no whisper of financial scandal has ever come near a Swiss insurance company. Very few Swiss banks have failed, but not one Swiss insurance company has failed.

Switzerland also holds some other world records in the insurance industry. For instance, the Swiss have the highest degree of insurance coverage in the world. The volume of Swiss insurance has generally been over 7% of GNP. Swiss insurers also span the longest time without a failure.

Swiss insurance companies are even safer than Swiss banks, precisely because the insurance companies are not allowed to conduct any kind of risky business. Their holdings are required, by law, to include only gilt-edged Swiss bonds and domestic real estate. Even then, relatively recent (1989) Swiss legislation limits the percent of capital that may be placed in Swiss real estate by insurance companies to a maximum of 30%.

Compare this to U.S. banks and insurance companies which jumped on the real estate bull market of the 1970s and 19802, only to end up holding a portfolio of problem real estate loans in the 1990s. Although Swiss real estate has held its value well, unlike the boom-bust cycle of many other real estate markets, the conservative Swiss wanted to make sure no Swiss insurance company endangered their credit by investing too heavily in the domestic real estate market.

The largest single holding of Swiss insurance companies is Swiss bonds. These bond portfolios are routinely carried on the books at market value, not cost, whereas real estate loans are often valued at cost, which could be less than half their current market value. Swiss conservatism comes through once again. With Swiss insurance companies, the insured person is even protected against overcharging. Nowhere else is money safer than in a Swiss insurance company. This success is not just due to strict regulation, but to the qualities of financial prudence, conservatism and sobriety which are bred into every Swiss citizen from birth.

The famous Swiss "hidden" reserves apply to insurance companies as well as banks. A recent Swiss insurance company audit demonstrated that fact. In order to see how Swiss insurance companies would measure up to the new European Union auditing standards, this company's shareholder's equity was audited from three different perspectives. As reported in *The Financial Times of London*, the results of these three accounting standards were as follows:

Shareholder's Equity	**As measured by:**
2.66 billion Swiss francs	Traditional Swiss standards
3.70 billion Swiss francs	Prevailing European accounting standards
4.64 billion Swiss francs	New EU accounting stan dards

In this example, the typical Swiss insurance firm under examination would have had more than one billion Swiss francs of excess assets, by prevailing European accounting standards, and nearly two billion Swiss francs of excess assets if measured by the new EU accounting standards. Nearly all major Swiss insurance companies have underestimated their true net worth along these lines.

That means a major depression or deflation could strike all the world markets and the Swiss insurance firms would have room to lose up to half the book value of their assets and still be solvent and able to meet all their financial obligations.

In the next chapter we will discuss some of the typical investments available through most Swiss insurance firms.

Chapter Five

The Revolutionary Swiss Asset Protection Certificate -The World's Safest Financial Account

"You may like to stay at home, but your portfolio shouldn't. Global diversification is always a good idea."

--Fortune magazine

Any sound investment portfolio should spread risk across a number of borders, industries and currencies, in order to minimize risk and maximize one's earnings potential. With safety and security for your investments increasingly difficult to find at home, international diversification is a must.

The Swiss Asset Protection Certificate (APC) is a vehicle to protect your assets and your family's financial well-being in times such as these. It provides all the privacy you want, but unlike a bank account, privacy is not the essential ingredient to protect your assets. The Certificate has a built in asset protection device. This device is in full legal compliance, has been tested in court and generally accepted for decades.

You'll be pleasantly surprised that the asset protection of your Certificate comes at no extra cost. Protection is a matter of law. This is a windfall when you think that setting up an offshore trust could easily cost you $20,000 in legal fees upfront and some percentage of every subsequent transfer!

Cost is just one benefit over offshore trusts. Another is, unlike trusts, the investor remains the legal owner of the investment. You never have to relinquish control of your assets. This also makes it much simpler to liquidate, which one can do at any time before the scheduled maturity. Any time you need it.

But as with any asset protection device, APCs are only valid if they are designed to protect against future, unanticipated litigation — not existing or threatened ones. Transfers occurring in view of the latter are deemed fraudulent.

"This Swiss Asset Protection Certificate is a fool-proof protective device"

How it works

The Swiss Asset Protection Certificate is actually an annuity. JML Swiss Investment Counsellors has redesigned the policy so that it meets all the requirements for a fool-proof asset protection device.

The basis of asset protection in Swiss life or annuity insurance policies is a provision in Swiss law that shields insurance investments from collection and bankruptcy procedures if the policy owner designates his sposue or children as beneficiaries. Or the owner may designate other parties, if done on an irrevocable basis. The idea is if you, as the owner, go bankrupt, ownership is automatically transferred to the beneficiaries who are beyond the reach of creditors.

Underlying all this is the traditional Swiss principle that everyone is entitled to protect their wealth for the benefit of family members. Not just the super-rich who can afford to pay hefty legal fees.

That may not be as romantic a proposition as it sounds. The pragmatic Swiss believe that the more wealth kept in the family, the less need for welfare programs. So until, welfare reformers everywhere come to this same conclusion, there will be a need for Swiss Asset Protection Certificates.

Why go overseas for asset protection? And why Switzerland?

First of all, it's important to go overseas for asset protection because this is the only way your assets can be placed beyond the reach of the legal, political and economic system you live in. In the U.S. in particular, the loss of financial privacy is a major concern. Your local trust company´s records can be summoned by government agencies and courts, anyone can learn the details of your bank account, your investments, even how you spend money. Your wealth is rendered visible — therefore vulnerable to all sorts of predators who might picture you as a potential vehicle for quick profit. In many countries, tax and exchange control systems punish investors to the point of confiscation.

For full lawsuit protection, investments must be made outside an investor´s legal jurisdiction — and inside a long-established, politically stable country that protects a person´s privacy and discourages frivolous and inventive litigation.

Now we come to Switzerland. It´s been around long enough (more than 700 years!) and kept at peace with its neighbors for many centuries. No mean feat for the war torn 20th Century. A financial infrastructure has existed since the Middle Ages, with traders´need for loans and deposit-taking giving rise to banking institutions. Due to its central location in Europe, those Swiss banks had an international clientele early on.

It is not by coincidence that Switzerland has the world´s toughest confidentiality and financial secrecy laws. It certainly did not happen overnight as in many offshore financial centers. Even before secrecy and asset protection laws came into existence, confidentiality had been the Swiss banker´s byword for generations. Indeed, privacy is part of the Swiss culture — your financial affairs are deemed to be your private business, and yours only.

We´ve already mentioned about how Swiss law provides for asset protection in Swiss life insurance policies. To summarize, as long as your spouse or children, or a third party when done irrevocably, are named as beneficiaries, your policy is protected. No bankruptcy court can then force you to redeem the policy. Your beneficiary need only inform the insurance company of the situation and the court´s action would be deemed a circumvention of Swiss rules.

Now we still have to mention how Swiss law discourages frivolous litigation. There´s enough here to fill a few comparative law books, but for now it should suffice to say that there are no contingency fee-based lawyers in Switzerland. So anyone who wants to crack at your nest egg, will have to pay up front for legal counsel. And since your Certificate also *offers you legal insurance* in Switzerland, you won´t need to put up a legal defense fund.

The Achilles Heel of asset protection trusts is something called "fraudulent conveyance". Is it the same for the Asset Protection Certificate?

Swiss law makes a similar ruling: transferring funds into an APC when litigation is pending which could make you insolvent, and doing so with your beneficiaries´ knowledge of your intent to defraud creditors, makes your APC null and void under Swiss fraudulent conveyance rules. The same is true in the case of a bankruptcy or judgment of asset seizure within 12 months, so long as the owner was solvent and no creditors has asserted any claims which would have rendered him or her insolvent at the time of designating the beneficiaries, then creditors are out of luck.

The smart thing to do is, as always, plan ahead. The next 12 months could be the difference between financial health and ruin.

Chapter Six

The Swiss Banking System -- An Oasis of Financial Security

"Money alone does not make you happy. You must have some of it in Switzerland, too."

-- *An old German proverb*

One major difference which has always set Switzerland apart from financial markets elsewhere is its established international outlook. This attitude is the product of generations of experience banking across borders -- originally with Switzerland's direct neighboring countries, France, Germany, Italy and Austria and, as history unfolded, as bankers to the world.

The Swiss banking and financial system has been successfully operating, essentially in its present form, serving the nations of Europe as long ago as the Middle Ages. Since World War II, Switzerland has gained worldwide recognition as the undisputed, leading financial "haven" for capital in search of protection when countless individuals and governments sought out Switzerland as a refuge for their assets during the unpredictable times of war.

Today, Switzerland is one of the top three financial centers of the world, after New York and London. Swiss banks manage over 2 trillion Swiss francs (Sfr. 2,150,000,000,000!), which equals approximately 1.4 trillion U.S. dollars! However, this is not surprising for a country that has made banking and finance management its major industry.

Switzerland is home to several hundred banking institutions ranging from small regional banks, to highly respected private banks and crowned by "The Big Three" -- Switzerland's AAA-rated Union Bank of Switzerland, Credit Suisse, and Swiss Bank Corporation. There are only four AAA-rated banks in the entire world and Switzerland is home to three of them. (The fourth is the Deutsche Bank of Germany.) The major Swiss banks also have branch offices in most of the world's financial centers from New York to Panama.

Strict Control Assures High Quality

Swiss banks are regarded as extremely safe institutions. The entire Swiss financial industry is tightly regulated and Swiss banks are strictly supervised by the Swiss Banking commission. Swiss banks face regular exacting and complex audits. The audit process is both comprehensive and meticulous. There are only 17 audit firms --

each approved by the Banking Commission -- which must follow a specific set of detailed procedures and rules laid down by the Banking Commission as they go over the banks' books. Because of its preciseness, the audit has become a guarantee for Swiss bank depositors.

There has never been a need for a Swiss equivalent of the U.S. Federal Deposit Insurance Corporation (FDIC) to bail out failing institutions. Liquidity and capital requirements for the operation of Swiss banks are also included in the banking law. Although quite complex, the results of the liquidity formula are clear: many Swiss banks maintain liquidity at or close to 100%. This is virtually unheard of in the banking systems of other nations. Also, in Swiss banks, 7% to 9% of the total liabilities must be equity. Compared to other countries, this is a high percentage. To prevent banks from having unrealized paper losses on its securities, Swiss banks that own securities must write them down to market, or cost (whichever is lower) every month. In the banks of other countries, unrealized paper losses are common, which conceals the banks' weakness. The formula for capital requirements and liability in Swiss banks results in strength and soundness of the entire banking system.

Universal Banking At Its Best

During the 1930s many nations, including the United States, began to distinguish between deposit banks and investment banks. This trend toward specialization is still apparent in the U.S. where not all banks offer all financial services. The Swiss, on the other hand, retained "universal" banking, in which banks offer just about any financial service there is. A typical Swiss bank can offer current, deposit and savings accounts, precious metals accounts, short-, long-term, and fiduciary deposits, stocks and bonds, mutual funds, mortgages, loans, etc. -- basically being a stock broker, commercial lender and investment bank also providing services in financial planning.

By providing all the services that any investor may need, by guaranteeing financial solidity and privacy and through their solid reputation for professional service, Swiss banks have gained worldwide influence and have created a climate in which an investor can have the highest degree of confidence -- a situation unequaled elsewhere in the world.

Swiss Bank Secrecy: The Banking Act of 1934

It was the French prelate-statesman Cardinal Richelieu who said: "Secrecy is the first essential in the affairs of state."

The rise to power of Adolf Hitler in Germany in 1933 was rightly viewed in Switzerland as a real threat to independence. The 1934 banking law was enacted to stop Nazi agents from bribing bank employees for information concerning the Swiss accounts of German citizens and expatriates but it still works today protecting foreign depositors from unwarranted intrusions into their banking privacy from any source. The Swiss government has steadfastly defended banking secrecy, in more recent times even against great foreign pressure to abandon it, usually from the official agencies of other governments.

Few people truly understand the nature and extent of Swiss privacy laws and regulations. They believe that Swiss secrecy makes the country a haven for "dirty" money, and that the Swiss have constructed obstacles to hinder law enforcement agencies from obtaining the evidence needed to prosecute criminals effectively. Then there are those who have come to believe that Swiss secrecy has deteriorated and doesn't exist anymore. Neither of these positions is true.

According to Swiss civil law, the information about a customer and his or her finances and investments is protected as a part of the individual's right to privacy. This has been made a part of Article 28 of the Swiss Civil Code. It not only protects the information, but places the burden of paying damages on any person who violates the privacy of another. Further, as noted earlier, the banking law provides severe penalties for a bank employee who divulges information about a customer. Any bank employee who does give information about a customer faces fines or imprisonment. The employee and his or her bank can be subject to penalties should a violation of privacy occur.

Only when authorized under existing statutory provisions, or by a Swiss court order, can a bank legally disclose information about a customer. Indeed, privacy is interpreted in such a manner that it is illegal for a bank to confirm whether or not an individual is even a customer.

While banking personnel are prevented from making disclosures of the financial dealings of their customers, the customers, of course, can authorize the banks to make certain information available. For example, the customer can waive secrecy and ask the bank to provide a credit reference to a specific creditor. Such waivers, however, are valid only if the customer's request is voluntary and he or she has not acted under duress. No one but the customer can waive secrecy.

On the other hand, Swiss secrecy is not absolute. Some specific statutory provisions can take precedence over privacy. These statutes usually have a limited scope, however, and concern Swiss inheritance law, the enforcement of judgments from creditors, and in cases of bankruptcy or divorce. Criminal investigations are another area where privacy can be overridden.

If a Swiss citizen commits a crime, criminal investigators can ask through a court order that secrecy is lifted. Treaties that Switzerland has with other countries extend this possibility to foreign crimes committed by foreign citizens, but the degree to which privacy may be set aside is limited by the language of each treaty. Foreign authorities can't directly request financial information from a Swiss financial institution about any customer. The authorities must first obtain a Swiss court order.

Certain conditions must be met before the Swiss will honor any request that affects privacy:

(1) In the case of criminal acts, the offense being prosecuted is considered to be a criminal offense in both the requesting country and in Switzerland.

(2) In cases regarding taxes, a disclosure of information is possible only if the investigation of the foreign tax law violation would also be considered a violation under Swiss law. There is a special provision between the Swiss and the United States (the Swiss-United States Treaty on Mutual Assistance in Criminal Matters) that provides for Swiss legal assistance to U.S. prosecutors in tax evasion cases when the investigation involves a suspected member of organized crime.

(3) The information obtained in Switzerland through a legal assistance procedure, generally, may not be used for investigative purposes, nor may it be introduced as evidence in the requesting state in any matter other than the specific offense for which the assistance was originally granted.

Although financial privacy is not absolute in Switzerland -- for the obvious necessities regarding criminal matters -- the rules and traditions governing it are solid and clearly defined.

Using the Services of Swiss Banks

Swiss banks are certainly a valuable institution for many of your Swiss-based investments. Banks provide some services not available through Swiss insurance companies. Swiss banks are different from U.S. banks in several regards, but when it comes to investment options their special services stand out.

Chapter Seven

Getting Started in Switzerland

"Money alone does not make you happy. You must have some of it in Switzerland, too."

-- *An old German proverb*

There are many choices awaiting an American investor in Switzerland. In order to help you choose intelligently, begin by identifying your goals. First of all, are you primarily interested in capital growth, funds to provide for your family, or funds for retirement?

If **CAPITAL GROWTH** is your main goal, you then must know the degree of risk you are willing to tolerate. Here are some options:

For an investment free of market and price risks, establish a Swiss Plus account.

For a diversified investment with a moderate level of risk, managed on your behalf by a team of Swiss and international managers, establish a MASTER managed portfolio account with a Swiss bank.

If **PROVIDING FOR YOUR FAMILY** is your main goal, you can choose a combined insurance-investment plan:

For life insurance coverage, combined with cash accumulation, purchase a Swiss endowment policy.

If **PROVIDING FOR RETIREMENT** is your main goal, you can choose between two options:

For guaranteed income, free of market or price risk, purchase a Swiss income annuity.

For a higher income, but with slightly greater market and price risk, establish a bond portfolio account with a Swiss bank.

Enlisting the Help of Swiss Experts

For an international investor, seeking the safety of Switzerland, there are many ways to proceed. You may contact individual banks, investment managers and insurance companies. But in many cases, language difficulties will complicate the selection process. Ideally, an investor should consult with several independent experts before investing overseas. It would be ideal, for instance, to have a few Swiss bank directors as friends and confidantes, maintain a hotline to insurance and finance companies, and be an exclusive client of an international tax expert. Best of all, this advice and information should all be available to you for no cost!

That's the ideal. The reality is that most people have no such access. Even rich and powerful investors, who have access to the best information, cannot keep track of all the information that comes their way. That's why most investors need a one-stop source of key information from many financial disciplines.

For this reason, non-Swiss investors who are interested in any of the investments discussed in this report, should use the services of a long established firm familiar with all these investment options, JML Swiss Investment Counsellors, based in Zurich, the firm that developed the Swiss Asset Protection Certificate.

JML Swiss Investment Counsellors has been in business since 1974 (and their first customer is still a satisfied customer). Since then, well over 20,000 clients have sent a portion of their wealth to grow in value, Swiss style. These JML clients currently hold over 3.5 billion Swiss francs in Swiss annuities and Swiss managed investment accounts.

The founder and President of JML, Jurg M. Lattmann, has been interviewed by *Forbes, The New York Times, The Wall Street Journal* and several other major publications in regard to his unique Swiss investment products designed for American investors. He is a widely published author in two languages. His German-language book, **Das Buch vom Geld** ("The Money Book") was a best-seller in Germany.

From JML, you can get independent information and advice on the best Swiss banks, insurance companies and investment programs to fit your needs, along with counsel on both Swiss and U.S. tax and privacy laws. And it costs you nothing.

JML is independent because they are not your contractual partner, and never will be. Your financial partners are the Swiss banks and insurance companies with which you deposit your funds. JML's services are to help investors find the most appropriate balance of investment products to fulfill their investment needs.

JML offers a Swiss perspective on a U.S. investors' needs -- to find the best possible yield, with the highest possible security. Asking JML for advice costs no more than going to the contractual party directly, and with several other advantages:

JML services are free. You don't pay for the services of JML, because JML is paid by the insurance firms and banks in which they place your accounts. Furthermore, JML is not restricted by conflicts of interest with any specific companies. All Swiss insurance commissions are standardized and are tightly regulated by the Swiss authorities. JML has no incentive to select one company over another, except to give JML clients the best possible service.

JML holds no client funds. All payments are made directly to Swiss banks or Swiss insurance companies.

JML offers investors a single overseas address for a wide variety of investment programs -- insurance, banking, annuities, gold managed funds and more. JML constantly monitors the Swiss financial markets for each of them.

Everyone at JML speaks English. From the receptionist to the account managers, everyone speaks excellent English. They also understand how an American IRA or Keogh plan works. They have answers to many of your U.S. **or** Swiss tax questions. They know all of the little details that are of no importance to Swiss investors but may be critical for you.

They stay open late (until 6:00 pm, which is 12:00 noon, EST) to serve Americans by telephone or telefax (available 24 hours).

Personal service. You can visit JML in Zurich. You can write them, call them and get to know their staff (there are only 15 of them) on a personal basis. They'll never grow too big to lose that personal touch.

The information you submit to JML will, of course, be treated in absolute confidence in accordance with Swiss law, which makes it a crime to disclose such financial information to any third party. JML will analyze your requirements and will respond to you by airmail promptly.

For further information contact:

JML Swiss Investment Counsellors

Germaniastrasse 55, Dept. 212

CH-8033 Zurich, Switzerland

Phone: (011) +41 1 368-8233 (from the U.S.)

FAX: (011) +41 1 368-8299;

marking your fax "attn: Dept. 212"

You may also write to the address above to request that you be added to the mailing list for a free subscription to *Swiss Perspective*, a monthly newsletter (usually 6 or 8 pages) with information on global trends and investment strategies, as well as news on Switzerland.

About The Author

Nicholas van Rijn has written for a wide variety of publications, from *Financial Freedom Report* to *Business Opportunities Journal*, and *The Christian Science Monitor*.

www.ingramcontent.com/pod-product-compliance
Ingram Content Group UK Ltd.
Pitfield, Milton Keynes, MK11 3LW, UK
UKHW012247290726
14090UKWH00013B/510

9 780894 990281